I0762604

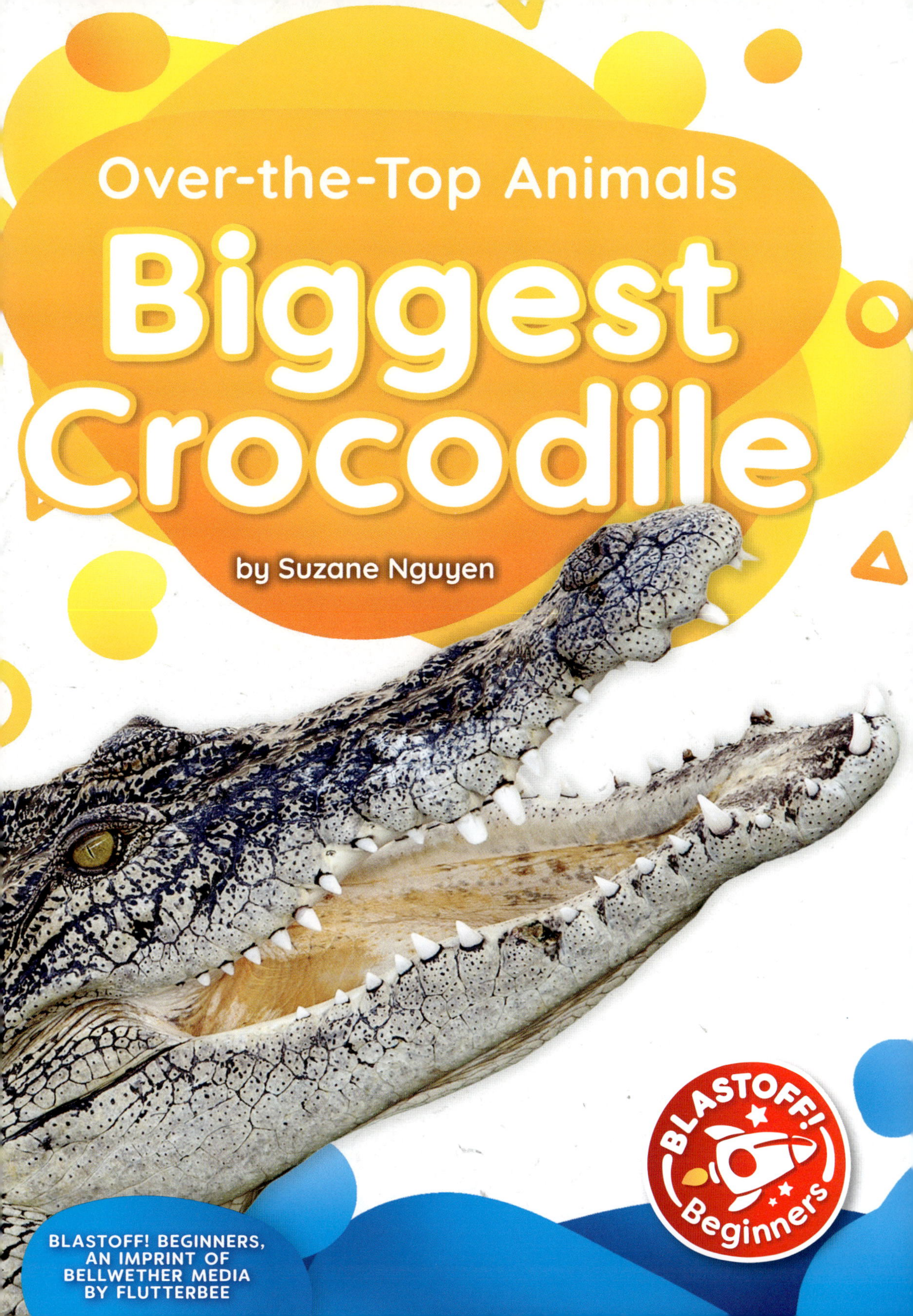
Over-the-Top Animals
Biggest Crocodile
by Suzane Nguyen
BLASTOFF! BEGINNERS, AN IMPRINT OF BELLWETHER MEDIA BY FLUTTERBEE
BLASTOFF! Beginners

**Blastoff! Beginners** are developed by literacy experts and educators to meet the needs of early readers. These engaging informational texts support young children as they begin reading about their world. Through simple language and high frequency words paired with crisp, colorful photos, Blastoff! Beginners launch young readers into the universe of independent reading.

## Sight Words in This Book

| | | | | |
|---|---|---|---|---|
| a | have | see | them | use |
| and | help | than | these | water |
| are | it | the | they | |
| big | long | their | too | |

This edition first published in 2027 by Bellwether Media, Inc.



For information regarding permission, write to Bellwether Media, Inc., Attention: Permissions Department, 3500 American Blvd W, Suite 150, Bloomington, MN 55431.

Library of Congress Cataloging-in-Publication Data is available at www.loc.gov or upon request from the publisher.

ISBN: 9798898800208 (hardcover)
ISBN: 9798898801441 (ebook)

Editor: Betsy Rathburn Designer: Laura Sowers

Printed in the United States of America, North Mankato, MN.

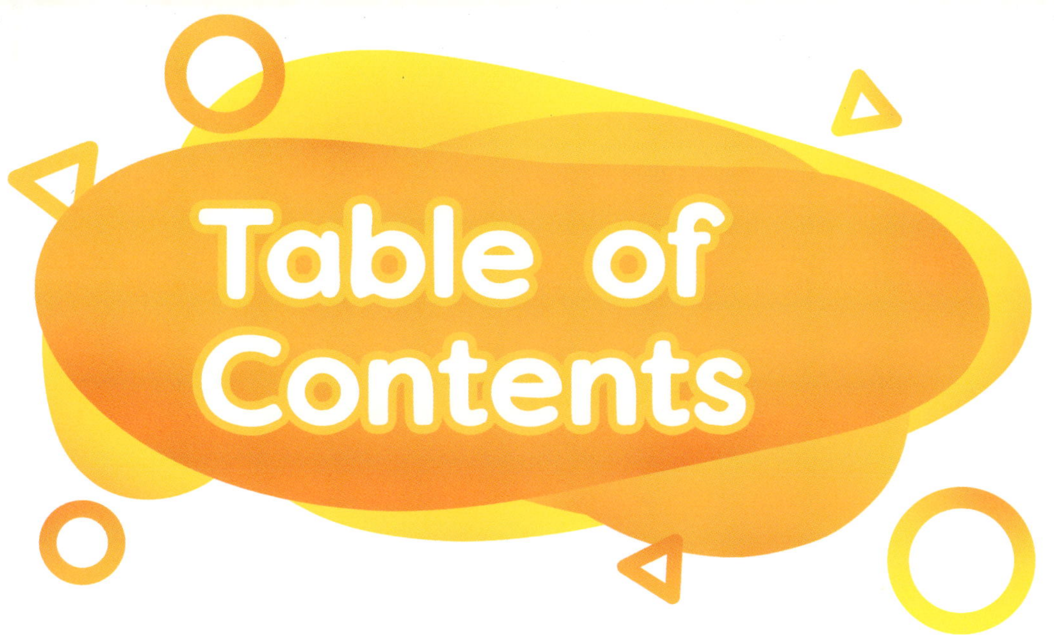
Table of Contents

# Hungry Hunter

A crocodile
sees its meal.
Snap!
It bites hard!

Saltwater crocodiles are the biggest **reptiles**.

They are longer than a car!

They have
long **snouts**.
They have
long tails too.

tail
snout

They have strong **jaws**. Their teeth are big.

teeth

jaw

# Strong Swimmers

Crocodiles use their size. Their long snouts catch small meals.

They hunt
big meals too.
Strong jaws and
big teeth help.

They swim fast. Long tails help them **steer**.

These reptiles rule land and water!

# The Biggest Crocodile

## Body Parts

## Using Their Size

catch small animals

eat big animals

swim fast

# Glossary

**jaws**: strong bones that let animals bite

**reptiles**: cold-blooded animals that lay eggs

**snouts**: noses and mouths

**steer**: to control movement

# To Learn More

## ON THE WEB

## FACTSURFER

Factsurfer.com gives you a safe, fun way to find more information.

1. Go to www.factsurfer.com.
2. Enter "biggest crocodile" into the search box and click 🔍.
3. Select your book cover to see a list of related content.

# Index




The images in this book are reproduced through the courtesy of: SanchaiRat, front cover; Danny Ye, p. 3; Jamesbowyer, pp. 4-5; sushil kumudini chikane, pp. 6-7; rweisswald, pp. 8-9; David Wall/ Alamy Stock Photo, pp. 10-11; infocusvideo, p. 12; Kim, pp. 12-13; LouieLea, pp. 14-15; Lauren Suryanata, pp. 16-17; Minden Pictures/ SuperStock, pp. 18-19; Pius Rino Pungkiawan, pp. 20-21; dwi putra stock, p. 22; AustralianCamera, p. 22 (catch small animals); Universal Images/ SuperStock, p. 22 (eat big animals); micahwgentry, p. 22 (swim fast); RealityImages, p. 23 (jaws); Tomgc/ Wirestock Creators, p. 23 (reptiles); Nantapong Kittisubsi, p. 23 (snouts); Svitlana, p. 23 (steer).